doll
Photo Shoot
Tips and tricks for amazing doll pics!

by Trula Magruder

★ American Girl®

Published by American Girl Publishing
Copyright © 2014 American Girl

Questions or comments? Call 1-800-845-0005, visit americangirl.com, or write to Customer Service, American Girl, 8400 Fairway Place, Middleton, WI 53562-0497.

Printed in China
14 15 16 17 18 19 20 LEO 10 9 8 7 6 5 4 3 2 1

All American Girl marks are trademarks of American Girl.

Editorial Development: Trula Magruder
Art Direction: Lisa Wilber
Production: Jeannette Bailey, Judith Lary, Paula Moon, Kristi Tabrizi
Set Stylist: Kim Sphar
Doll Stylists: Emelia Haglund, Karen Timms
Photographers: Joe Hinrichs, Dawn Sabin
Photography: p. 7—© iStockphoto.com/Imgorthand;
p. 11—© iStockphoto.com/Spanic; p. 25—© iStockphoto.com/cunparis

Dear Doll Lover,

Capture your doll's first cartwheel. Shoot the smile she wore on her first day of school. Snap her expression at her surprise birthday party. Inside this book, you'll find photography tips and inspirational examples for taking dreamy, dramatic, and dazzling doll pics.

But before you start, learn how to operate your digital camera. Ask an adult to go over your camera's functions with you if you don't know how to use them.

Then study the professional advice on how to shoot, style, and craft award-winning doll scenes.

After that, practice your photography and set-building skills by completing the practice projects inside.

And finally, shoot, shoot again, and shoot some more. Use your artistic eye to show the world exactly why your doll is so special.

An AG doll stylist preps a doll for the shoot.

For even more fun, take your photography skills to the next level. Read the *Lights, Camera, Action!* manual inside to learn how to shoot stop-action videos of your doll!

Your friends at American Girl

CRAFT WITH CARE

Keep Your Doll Safe

When making props or wardrobe, remember that dyes from ribbons, felt, beads, cords, fabrics, fleece, and other supplies may bleed onto your doll or her clothes and leave permanent stains. So use lighter colors when possible, and check your doll often to make sure the colors aren't transferring to her body, her vinyl, or her clothes. And never get your doll wet! Water and heat increase dye rub-off.

Craft Smart

Ask an adult to approve all craft supplies before you use them—some are not safe for kids.

Keep Little Kids Away

If you stop in the middle of a shoot, keep your set, supplies, and equipment off-limits to kids and pets!

SET SMARTS

Kit Supplies

Use the clear rubber bands so your doll can hold props. Slip one over her wrists, and remove it right after your shoot. Delete the rubber band from your picture with a photo-editing software, or leave it in—we've done both in this book! Slip your best photos in the album and frame, or attach them to the photo cards. For silly snaps, add the stickers. And shoot your doll in front of the posters for cool backdrops. Be sure to fill the frame with the image. For more doll fun, read the stop-action manual, *Lights, Camera, Action!*, and make a movie!

Protect Your Doll

When shooting with a light source, snap the photo and turn off the light IMMEDIATELY. Lamps, studio lights, and reflecting boards can heat your doll and quickly melt her vinyl. Don't bring your doll out in the rain, play with her in the sand or snow, or leave her in the sun for long periods of time.

Ask First!

Before shooting at ANY location—even the backyard—ask an adult if it's OK to do so.

Candids

Pose your doll to look as if she doesn't know you're there!

Don't Look Now!

In candid pictures, people seem spontaneous and true to life. To create your own candids, pose your doll as if she were doing something while you weren't around, and then suddenly— *snap!*—you captured her in action.

Pro Tips

• When shooting a scene, use a tripod. This allows you to adjust the props, lighting, and doll without changing the image in your frame.

• Imitate poses and positions from photos of people.

• Adjust your doll's head, arms, and legs so that they look like you've captured them mid-motion.

• Shoot pics from lots of angles. Then choose your favorites, and delete the rest.

• Give your doll something to interact with by adding another doll, a pet, or a prop.

📷 Re-create a candid picture someone took of you. Place your doll where you were in the picture.

Portraits

Focus on the face when planning a portrait.

Face Her

A portrait should focus on your doll as the subject, and it should reveal who she is (at least to you) as much as possible. When capturing your doll's portrait, always make sure her eyes are in focus.

Pro Tips

- Move the camera in so close that you can see the light in your doll's eyes or the freckles on her face.

- Use props to reveal more about your doll's personality.

- Ask someone to hold a light over your doll's head to make her hair shine.

📷 Frame your doll's face in an extreme close-up. Use the frame in your kit!

📷 Explore dramatic lighting. Use light shining through blinds to create interesting shadows.

📷 Shoot a full-body portrait of your doll from an unusual angle.

Groups

Bring in buddies to add story and interest.

Follow the Crowd

Whether you were at summer camp or a sleepover, you likely saw someone snapping group pictures. Shooting your doll in similar scenes can add interest and humor to your pics. If you have only one doll, ask your friends to bring their dolls to your shoot. And don't forget plush pets! Just as in real life, animals add charm to pictures.

Pro Tips

• Remove any people-sized props, footprints, or shadows.

• Move the dolls so that they chat, wave, or sit up to get a better view —just as you and your pals do!

• Place the dolls in scenes that real people would be shown in.

• Figure out how you can position the dolls so that their heights vary for visual interest.

practice project: wow with a crowd

📷 Play with evening light. Create an inspiring silhouette by shooting your dolls at dusk with the setting sun at their backs.

Outdoors

Step outside to light really lovely scenes.

Know the Sun

You don't need fancy studio lights to take stunning doll shots, but you do need great light. Sunlight is free and looks fantastic in photos—if you know how to use it. When working in the sun, you need to learn when the sun will create odd shadows or wash out colors. You need to know how to reflect light into the dark areas of your scene or dodge light in the overly bright areas. You also need to decide whether it's best to shoot in the shade, in the early-morning sun, in the late-afternoon sun, or on a cloudy day.

Pro Tips

- For richer colors, shoot just after sunrise or just before sunset. For softer light, shoot on a cloudy day or in the shade.

- To dodge light from a really bright area, block the sun with a black poster board.

- To add light to an area of your scene or your doll's face, make a reflection board. Cover a large poster board with aluminum foil, or use a white poster board. Ask someone to angle the board near the dark area or face—if you're alone, prop it up. You may need more than one board.

Move your doll into the shade, but use a reflector board or white poster board to bounce sunlight onto her face, hair, or entire body!

Shoot your doll in harsh sunlight, but filter the light by shading her with a white umbrella or tree leaves.

Indoors

Control your climate by shooting inside.

Step Inside

If you'd like to set up a photo studio, review the questions below with a parent. If he or she says yes to them, start planning your space!

- Is there a place in our home where pets and little kids can't enter?

- Can I use an area near a window or have access to lamps or spotlights?

- Can I create sets? If so, is there a desk, tabletop, or floor space I can arrange them on?

- Can I hang, drape, or arrange backdrops?

- **Safety warning:** Turn off your spotlights or lamps until you're ready to shoot—and then turn them off immediately after you've taken your shot. *Always* cover up your reflectors when you're not using them so that the sun doesn't continue to reflect and overheat your doll, walls, or room!

Pro Tips

- Typical studio lighting is called *three-point lighting*. (See the image below.) Note: the backlight can also be above your doll, and the key (main) light can be the sun shining through a window.

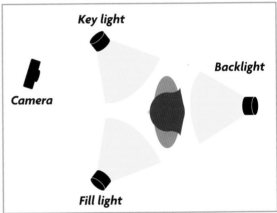

- Experiment with your lights. Different sets or poses may need different arrangements. Light your doll, and then move on to lighting the scene or set.

- Use a reflector board to angle the light from a nearby window onto your doll or scene.

- If you can, shoot in a room with white or light-colored walls. They reflect the light back onto your scene better.

Pose your doll in front of a colorful poster or paper cutout. Show her hugging a stuffed animal or another doll. Glue the photo onto a card from your kit, and write, "Just a little hug for you!" Give it to someone special.

Zoom

Step in closer to fill your frame.

Get in Close

Beginning photographers tend to stand too far from their subjects—and this often means boring pics. When shooting your doll, step in close to fill your camera's entire frame. Train yourself to check the edges of your viewfinder to remove anything that detracts from your doll or the scene. If you find a distraction, see if stepping in closer removes it.

Pro Tips

- Experiment with the zoom button on your camera.

- The closer you are to your doll, the steadier the camera must be. Use a tripod if the shot looks blurry.

- Shoot, step closer, shoot, step closer, shoot, step closer. Then choose the best shot!

- Experiment with cutting the edges off your doll photos. But crop just above or below your doll's joints so that she doesn't look amputated.

- Before you shoot, scan every inch of the camera's frame. Look for things that are growing out of your doll's head, for fingerprints on the props, and for other potential photo bloopers.

📷 A *medium shot* is a photo that is taken from about the shoulders up. Try it with two dolls.

📷 For a worm's-eye view, shoot your doll so that she looks gigantic—as if a worm had a camera!

Prop Size

Create right-size miniatures for your scenes.

Think 33

To give your American Girl doll right-sized props, do the math! First, measure an object that you want to re-create for your doll, such as a book. Say a real book measures 9 inches high by 9 inches wide. Using a calculator, you'd multiply 9 by 0.33. Your answer would be 2.97 inches. That means you'd make your doll book about 3 inches wide and 3 inches high. Of course, not everything needs to be *exactly* 33 percent smaller. You might stumble upon an item that looks like a small version of something used in real life. For example, a toothpick can be turned into a darling doll pencil!

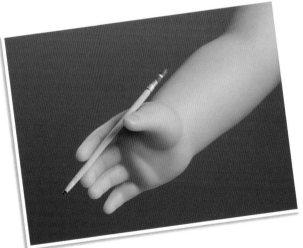

Pro Tips

- Look for 3-D scrapbook embellishments to enhance your scenes.

- Use a printer to reduce large flat items to 33 percent. Glue the copy to cardboard.

- Put stickers to work as art, wall décor, pictures, and more.

- Don't toss boxes, plastic packaging, and other containers. They make great doll furniture and household accessories.

- With permission, you can turn old mittens, socks, sleeves, and other clothing items into fashionable pieces.

practice project: make many minis

📷 Create lots of props for the set of an outdoor adventure. Then shoot your dolls in action!

Photo Sets

Design scenes and sets by studying real spaces and places.

Make the Scene

One way to make interesting photos is to shoot your doll in settings that imitate real places. Say you want to shoot your doll as if she were in *her* yard. You can't stand her in the tall grass near a bush in *your* yard—she'd look ridiculous. But if you were to pose her next to a houseplant in close-cropped grass, she'd seem natural to the scene. Still, it's OK to take artistic photos by posing your doll in unrealistic sets with fanciful props and backdrops. Or you can combine the two techniques. For example, you can shoot your doll watching a fake paper bird that's perched on a real tree branch!

AG stylists blow bubbles for an underwater scene.

Pro Tips

- To steady your doll for a long time in unstable positions, tie her wrists to clear fishing line that's secured overhead. Angle your camera so that the line is hidden or cut out of the frame. Or remove the line from your pic later with a photo-editing software.

- Make sure the outdoor terrain fits your doll's size. Try sand, pavement, or short-cut grass.

- You don't need to finish any part of the set that won't show in your picture!

- With permission, you can turn potted plants on their sides to create lush outdoor gardens.

- Fill empty spaces in your sets with interesting items. For instance, place a plush cat on a bare rug, or attach a small clock or picture to a plain wall.

practice projects: set the scenes

📷 Create a summer set, such as a farmer's market, and shoot your doll shopping.

📷 Build a fall set, such as a leaf-filled yard, and snap your doll raking.

📷 Design a winter set, such as a snow hill, and picture your doll swooshing by on skis.

📷 Make a spring set, such as a field of flowers, and shoot your doll flying the kite from your kit.

Model Styling

Make your doll dazzle with sweet styles and precious poses.

Looking Good

Styling your doll—whether you want her to look highly styled or natural—will give your photos more personality and power. Imagine that you've taken a gorgeous shot of your doll in a field of flowers, but her hair is sticking out on one side. Your viewer will spend more time noticing her hair than your pretty pic! By controlling your doll's appearance, you're choosing what you want the viewer to see. So pay attention to her clothes, hair, props, body position, and *eye line*—which means where the viewer thinks your doll is looking.

Pro Tips

- Style your doll's hair to fit the scene. Make sure her ponytail, bun, or a few loose hairs show on at least one side of her head, or her locks will look oddly cropped.

- Tilt your doll's head to give her instant personality.

- Don't show your doll's arms and legs in matching positions. Place one forward and one back or one up and one down.

- Press a loop of clear tape in your doll's hand, and she can hold her skirt hem or lightweight props.

- Just before you snap the pic, tug on your doll's outfit to remove wrinkles. Then smooth her stray hairs. You may need to spritz water on stubborn strays—but always shield her eyes with your hands or a cloth.

📷 Imagine that you've been hired to shoot an urban scene. Style your doll and a set to convey that place.

📷 Imagine you've been hired to shoot a paparazzi-style candid of a movie star. Style your doll and a set to show that moment.

Backgrounds

Add flavor and feeling to your shots
with strong settings.

Behind the Scenes

Beginning photographers often think that what's
in the background of a photo doesn't matter because,
well, it's in back. But look at the photo shown top right.
The doll is in a messy room with a girl-sized chair,
socks, and stuffed pets. Did you see the cute
doll props? Probably not.

What if the doll were in front of that purple wall
and the room was empty? Would you know what
the photographer wanted to show you? And how
long would you look at that picture? Too few
details can be as bad as too many.

Now look at the photo shown bottom right. You
see the chalkboard, move to the globe, and then
peer at the desk. You spot the books and study
the doll. You see just enough detail to reveal a
story—ah, the doll is a teacher in class!

Pro Tips

• Use real-life settings as backdrops, or make them
  from fabric, sheets, paper, or cardboard.

• Pay attention to the colors in your foreground and
  background. If they match, your doll may get lost.
  If they're very different, the shot might look busy.

• Sometimes, it's OK to blur the background or
  foreground—as long as your doll's in focus.

practice projects: watch your doll's back

📷 Photograph your doll in front of a glittery backdrop. Does it look wonderful or weird?

📷 Shoot your doll in front of a poster so that it looks like she's actually at that location. Hide the poster edges. Is the effect cool or crazy?

📷 Dress your doll in something that makes her blend into her background. Does she seem hip or hidden?

Wardrobe

To create a convincing picture, dress your doll correctly.

Fashion Your Scene

When it's 70 degrees in your studio, and your doll is making angels in fake snow, you might think it's OK to slip her into a pretty sundress—but don't. It's important to make the moment in your scene believable by showing your doll dressed to suit the season, time of day, and event—not the actual temperature inside or the season outside.

Pro Tips

• Stuff your doll's outfit with tissue paper or quilt batting to give it the shape you want.

• To remove wrinkles from doll clothes, hang them near a steamy shower, or ask an adult to iron them if the label says it's safe to do so.

• Don't allow clothing to steal the scene. If your doll's wearing a sparkly dress on a walk in the park, it'll distract your viewer from the moment you were trying to create.

• After you've dressed your doll for her scene, take a look at her from head to toe. If anything stands out too much, change it, or it'll stand out to your viewer, too.

• Don't forget accessories! If your doll's reading, think about glasses. If she's at a fancy party, consider jewelry. If she's on a bike, add a helmet.

• Before shooting, always check over your doll for loose threads, stray hairs, and specks of dust.

📷 Place your doll in a scene dressed as a character from one of your favorite books.

📷 Dress your doll and pose her for the cover of a fancy fashion magazine.

📷 For an interesting shot, fill your frame with fabric. "Drown" your doll in a pool of tulle or other fun fabric, and snap her picture.

📷 Shoot a picture of your doll dressed for a party. Ask friends to toss up confetti, and snap the pic while the pretty paper floats in the air!

Mistakes

Give crummy photos the respect they deserve.

Too Bad

It's fine to take a bad picture now and then —all pros do. But if you don't learn why your picture was bad or how it happened, you'll tend to make that mistake over and over again, and even with a digital camera, that can be frustrating. So when your doll's picture doesn't look quite right, investigate what went wrong. Try to repeat the shot to see if you can make the same mistake, ask an experienced photographer if she knows what the problem is, or share it with friends to see what they think. You can even start a club for sharing and critiquing doll pictures!

Pro Tips

- Spots on your shots? Don't touch the lens with your bare fingers, and before each shooting session, clean it with a soft, lint-free cloth.

- Scenes seem grainy? Photos can become dotted (or *pixilated*) in low light. If you can't improve the lighting, shoot on a tripod or use a flash.

- Odd composition? Leave extra space in the direction your doll is facing.

- Blurry pic? Reduce camera movement. Hold the camera firmly with both hands, place your right index finger over the shutter-release button, and gently press it. You can also use a tripod or a shutter-release cable.

- Wrong area in focus? Learn how to focus your camera manually or how to set your auto mode to what you want in focus—your doll!

📷 Shoot your doll on a tilted horizon (where the earth and sky meet), and then shoot her so that the frame and horizon line up. Which looks best?

📷 Shoot your doll smack in the middle of a scene, and then move her a little to the left in the scene. Which is more enjoyable to look at?

Tricks

Surprise viewers with jaw-dropping doll pics.

Special Shots

Take amazing doll photos! By increasing the distance between two subjects and controlling the placement of those subjects, such as the doll and the flower shown at right, you can shoot artistic, funny, or thought-provoking pictures. You can make one doll appear larger than another, show a doll holding up the moon, or even capture yourself standing in the palm of your doll's hand! Now who wouldn't want to see that?

Send a snapshot of your favorite doll picture to

Doll Photo Shoot Editor
8400 Fairway Place
Middleton, WI 53562

Sorry, but photos can't be returned. All comments and suggestions received
by American Girl may be used without compensation or acknowledgment.

Here are some other American Girl books you might like:

Discover online games, quizzes, activities,
and more at **americangirl.com**